T0208817

YOU
WANNA
RACE?

YOU
WANNA
RACE?

An Entry-Level Guide to Motorsports

JOE SCARBROUGH

YOU WANNA RACE?
AN ENTRY-LEVEL GUIDE TO MOTORSPORTS

iUniverse books may be ordered through booksellers or by contacting:

iUniverse
1663 Liberty Drive
Bloomington, IN 47403
www.iuniverse.com
1-800-Authors (1-800-288-4677)

Because of the dynamic nature of the Internet, any web addresses or links contained in this book may have changed since publication and may no longer be valid. The views expressed in this work are solely those of the author and do not necessarily reflect the views of the publisher, and the publisher hereby disclaims any responsibility for them.

Any people depicted in stock imagery provided by Thinkstock are models, and such images are being used for illustrative purposes only. Certain stock imagery © Thinkstock.

ISBN: 978-1-5320-1815-2 (sc)
ISBN: 978-1-5320-1816-9 (e)

Library of Congress Control Number: 2017905015

Print information available on the last page.

iUniverse rev. date: 04/06/2017

ACKNOWLEDGEMENTS

Before we begin, I would like to take a moment and thank the many family and friends who have contributed to my racing career.

First, I want to thank my longtime friend and fellow competitor, Wendy Drake, for her input and review of my rough works. "Gentleman Joe," my father, provided his support during the years of my driving career. "Iron Mike Rubino" provided great driving mentorship. John Palisi, John Matlach, and George Taylor gave all the lessons taught for the preparation of a race car. Chuck Hawks, a great coach, completed the package by tuning my mental focus on and off the track. Finally all of the team owners granted me the opportunity to pursue my dream in professional motorsports.

INTRODUCTION

If you are reading this, you probably have the ambition to participate in one of the greatest adrenaline-filled sports in the world, auto racing. I was born into a racing family, as some of you may also have been, and I have to warn you, once racing is in your blood, you cannot get it out. Racing is, in fact, such an addictive sport that it may be genetically transferred to your children, much the same way an alcoholic's kids are likely to drink! You have been warned. Turn back now, or enter at your own risk!

Over the course of my career, I have made many great friends in racing and unfortunately destroyed a few personal relationships. I have seen much of the same happen to many other racers. It all comes down to a prioritization of money and time. If you sell your living room furniture to buy race car parts or spend every waking moment in the race shop or at the racetrack, you are probably going to end up in divorce court! Moderation is key. Don't spend what you don't have, don't get lost in the racing world, and don't forget about the other aspects of your life. You will thank me for this later.

A little background information about me, I began racing at the ripe old age of ten in go-karts. Don't laugh! Karting, to this day, is still the fastest, highest G-force and the best bang for the buck in racing. I later moved onto full-sized cars, late model, super late model, street stock, modified, and even sports cars. I have collected close to 275 wins at dozens of tracks, ranging from the high banks of Daytona; the twisty mountain course of Laguna Seca; the bullring ovals of the East Coast like Wall Stadium in New Jersey; Bowman Gray in Winston-Salem, North Carolina; and almost all of the legendary short tracks of the Southeast. I have scored eight championships as a driver, two as a crew chief, and one as a car owner. I even managed to make a living racing—or at least in the network of racing—for the better part of my life. Even during my stint in the United States Coast Guard, I found myself behind the wheel of a Port Security intercept boat. For the most part, I have earned my living through opportunities made from my racing network of friends or my abilities behind the wheel. At this moment, I am managing a construction company for my friend who I met through my racing friends network and whose late model I drove at the famed Southside Speedway in Richmond, Virginia.

For thirty-seven years, I pursued racing as a career and did whatever I had to do to make ends meet. (No, I did not do anything immoral.) I rose through the ranks, as high as the NASCAR Touring Modified and Grand Am ST divisions. The problem for me, though, was by the time I got those opportunities, I was in my late thirties and early forties, not a place for an aging race car driver to be in an up-and-coming position. With a lack of personal funding, I found myself going back down the ladder, which turned out was really not such a bad place to be. I worked with some great people, I was blessed with team owners (who have become great friends), and I was still taking home my share of wins and championships.

In April 2015, I suffered a head injury that finally closed the deal for me. This was one of many head injuries throughout my life, but it has had some long-lasting effects, including memory loss, vision changes, and equilibrium issues. And some say that I did actually get a little dumber.

Two years prior to my final braining, I was at a crossroads in my racing career. I had decided to build an entry-level team that was capable of winning for under $10,000. (I didn't quite hit that number, but I was damn close.) I shopped and hunted parts and pieces for two years to put my last blast together. I restored a 1989 Dodge truck, bought an open trailer and a used car, and had an engine built for just over $11,000. Originally intending to be an owner/driver yet now retired, I made a deal with my longtime friend and defending track champion, Ryan Hutchens, to drive for my team. In our first season, we won four out of six races and finished first in the championship standings.

Going back to entry-level racing with the years of experience I have gained has really made me look at a lot of the entry-level racers and ask, "What the hell are you thinking?" Seeing some of the safety issues, lack of preparation, and general ignorance of the entry-level racer reminds me of my father's first death trap, or as we referred to it, "the race car."

Seeing firsthand the costly and sometimes dangerous mistakes the participants of this sport make inspired me to write a book of guidance. (Hopefully someone will read it.) Many people in this sport have a great passion for racing yet will not invest in the education required to improve their knowledge base. I could never understand a guy who runs in the back of the pack and yet refuses to accept advice from more knowledgeable people. And to top it off, they keep everything they do a secret! I have just come to love the line, "I've been doing this for twenty years." I am usually thinking in my screaming inside voice, "And you still haven't won a race!"

I know it is difficult, but from this point forward, you must leave your ego behind. Not just reading this book but forever after. Once you believe you know everything and there is no other possibility that it can be done better, you have begun to lose the game. I have taken great information away from teams that frankly couldn't find their butt with both hands but somehow managed to come up with one great idea!

One common mistake I have seen in every level of racing is people with a passion for the sport, who lack education of the sport, spend an ungodly amount of money to chase this addictive passion, often straight to the poorhouse and divorce court.

It is my intent to enlighten you as to the common, grand mistakes made at the entry level of racing, regardless of the type of racing: cars, motorcycles, boats, and so forth. Many of my references are about cars, but the basics are the same— knowledge, infrastructure, safety, funding, and fun!

LESSON 1

Pre-investment

You want to race! Why do you want to race? Think about this for a moment. It is very important that you ask yourself this question before you dive headfirst into it. If you have intentions of going to the top divisions of the largest sanctioning bodies, then, in my opinion, the only thing you should purchase is your personal safety gear and sign up for every driving school you can find. Once you have earned a competition license or sufficient training to enter a non-sanctioned event, start contacting teams willing to rent a full-service race operation that includes testing and coaching. The steps toward professional racing are not very difficult as long as you have the financing required to keep a race team in business. If you simply pay the bills and don't do anything stupid or malicious on or off track, you will make it up the ranks. It is not really about talent.

Don't get me wrong. I was one of the very few people able to make it fairly high on talent, only to be stonewalled by teams requiring me to shell out $35,000 or more per event to move up. Yes, that's how it works. If you believe that you are going to start your own team, move up in divisions, attract the grand sponsor, or have Roger Penske spy your talent from the grandstands or YouTube, then I would like to sell you a map that

1

has unicorn and Bigfoot locations on it. If your intention is to just get out there and race with no real expectations of winning the international driving championship, your participation in the sport will have a lot less stress. Just go out and have fun!

I often use my father as an example of what not to do when starting a race team. Despite the fact that my grandfather was a very competent car builder and mechanic, my dad asked him very little advice until he was buried in racing. No garage, no hauler, limited tools, and virtually no knowledge. Building a race car in the backyard based off a model car built by your nine-year-old son is not the way to start. Only after burnt eyes from welding, second-degree burns from a radiator hose that wasn't secured, a couple injuries from inadequate safety equipment, and years later, my father figured it out, won many races, and a couple championships. My dad learned to set up cars and drive them. My father also picked a lot of brains at the racetrack, mostly from the upper divisions, and he was wise enough to follow the instructions from one guy at a time. He picked the minds of legends like Richie Evans and Charlie Jarzombek. Racers in the division above yours are more likely to give you accurate information for two reasons. If they are really good at racing a more sophisticated machine than you, they likely have more knowledge. And they don't have to beat you on the racetrack so the information they give you is likely to be truthful and not misleading.

During the years of my father's growth, I had the advantage of learning from his mistakes without paying the price out of my own pocket. By the time I was fourteen, I was able to set cars up, perform most of the maintenance, weld, and even begin driving his late model in testing and practice sessions. With a seasoned driver (my dad) as a coach, combined with becoming his full-time crew chief, it granted me the advantage needed to hit the ground running when I did field my own team. In reality, I had been doing what I am telling you to do.

For the rest of us who have a passion for the sport and still need to work Monday through Friday, start on the spectator side of the fence. Do not run out and buy a race car! And for God's sake, don't build one! Doing this will be much more expensive and possibly dangerous. Let's face it. Whatever type of racing you are interested in competing in, the speeds exceed that which people are killed every day on the interstates and motorways. If you have already done so or may even be racing already, it's not too late. Park it and follow these instructions, and when you come back in your own car, it will be safer and faster.

Watch the teams with well-prepared cars. If the crew members are uniformed (and entry level usually means T-shirts), go over and introduce yourself. If you have begun racing already, you may already know them. Ask if the team needs help. If the team accepts you onto the roster, do everything you can to be involved during the week. Don't be intimidated by the fact that you may see twenty crew members at the racetrack. I'll bet the farm that, on a Wednesday at midnight, there aren't more than two people in the shop preparing and repairing the car for the next event. Be one of those guys! If you find resistance with teams in your own division, try the division above yours. Work with the team. Gain knowledge of the cars, the expenses, and the logistics. See if your family remembers who you are in the fall when the season is over. If you are lucky, your family will embrace the sport and enjoy it as much as you do. More importantly, you will be learning exactly what it takes and costs to run a winning operation.

Read! You have to study everything you can about racing. You should have at least one monthly subscription to a magazine that is geared toward your type of racing for one year prior to buying anything. You are about to learn a new language called "What does it cost, and where do I get it?" When you are reading your subscription and it has an article about "low-resistance muffler bearings," it is now time to translate that into "Can I still pay my mortgage if I buy one?"

Steps You Need To Take

1. Take your family to the racetrack and see how they like it. Talk to them about your desire to participate as a driver or owner.
2. Make a business plan and write down every projected expense. Most overlooked expenses are the consumables and greatest recurring expenses such as tires, race fuel, and fuel for the hauler.
3. Plan your next vacation to a driving school. Bandurant and Skip Barber are very famous names, but you can find many others in the world that align with your interest in racing, not to mention that I have a training program as well. Just because it isn't the same type of car or course does not mean you will not take away a great amount of knowledge from it. Road racers know how to shift and have amazing footwork. Oval racers learn left foot braking. The more diversified your education is, the better off you will be.

4. Take a welding class, especially if you intend to race oval track.

5. Volunteer for a successful race team at the track you intend to compete at. Spend as much time as you can with that team. Any time work is being done on that car (or with that team), you should be there. If the team is changing engines, be there. If the team is cleaning the shop, be there. If the team is setting the car up, you had better be there! What you will be learning is the time and devotion required to race as well as how to maintain and fix your own race car.

LESSON 2

Getting Started

It's time to start putting it all together. You have worked with a team. You know what your budget and expense of the division you intend to go into requires and the time involved to maintain a race team. Let's go buy a race car, right? No! Not right! Don't be that guy with a race car and no way to haul it, no place to park it, and no tools to work on it!

At one point in time, a team owner who wanted me to manage a brand-new team as well as drive the cars approached me.

This very eager team owner who was ready to dive in headfirst came to me and said, "I found a deal on a two-car team of Porsche 997s for $125,000!"

I responded, "You don't own a wrench!"

A pair of competitive Grand Am series GS Porsche 997's for $125,000 is a great deal, but the additional million dollars required to get the operation to the racetrack might have been a bit of a surprise!

Step One—Location! Location! Location!

Where do you intend to keep your car? A garage is damn nice to have! You will really appreciate it when Mother Nature decides to not cooperate. Don't get me wrong. You can do this in a driveway outdoors, but snow, rain, and summer heat can really make things difficult. Having an enclosed area will also shield the late-night noise you are bound to make. For some reason, the neighbors in my residential neighborhood didn't appreciate all the grinding and hammering late at night after a tough night at the racetrack.

If you have a garage at your home, you are going to need at least two bays. If it's a single-car garage, your tools will live inside, and the car will stay out. Most areas have industrial complexes reasonably close by and usually inexpensive. I do not encourage teaming up and sharing a shop. Trust me. It rarely if ever works out!

Step Two—Tools!

Lots of them! Get wrenches, sockets, hammers, electrical tools, air compressor, jack and stands, welder, rivet gun, diagnostic, and setup equipment. Unless you intend to tote your race car out to a repair facility every time something breaks, bends, or simply needs to be improved or set up, you need to be able to do all of this in-house. By working with that race team last year, you should know how to do this and be familiar with some knowledgeable people to help guide you through it.

Here is a start-up list of tools. If you are racing a car that is completely metric like most modern cars and imports, you probably will not need a standard set until your trailer fails.

- Markers, pencils, pens, and notepads
- Four wrench sets: two standard and two metric
- Two ratchet sets: ½ drive and 3/8 drive with metric and standard sockets
- Two impact socket sets: ½ drive, one metric, and one standard

- Two screwdriver sets: one standard and one Phillips
- Two Allen sets: metric and standard
- One hydraulic jack[1]
- Four jack stands[2]
- Hammers: a five-pound sledge and some planishing tools[3]
- Pry bars of various sizes
- Air pressure gauge
- Caster camber gauge
- Scales
- Tow plates
- String
- All the tape measures you can afford[4]
- Compressor and tools
- Welder, rivet gun, sheet metal shears, metal break, pipe bender, and so forth[5]
- Drain pan
- Torque wrench: ½ drive[6]
- Fire extinguishers[7]

---

[1] Don't skimp. Get a one-ton jack.

[2] Again, don't skimp. Get some nice, tall one-ton stands.

[3] You are bound to bend something eventually!

[4] Why? They disappear like socks!

[5] This all depends on how involved your fabricating gets. You can save a lot of money doing your own fabricating work, but I do not recommend fabricating anything that impacts the safety and integrity of your car. Making bumpers and body mounts are fine, but leave roll cage, seat, and suspension mounting to the professionals.

[6] Torque race car lugs after every run. Most cars require sixty-five to eighty-five pounds. Check with the manufacturer.

[7] Get as many as you can. You can't have too many: one on each wall in your shop, one in your truck, and one in your trailer. If the rulebook does not require an onboard fire suppression system in your car, get one anyway!

Step Three—Truck!

Reliable transportation is essential. It does not matter how good your race car is if it's sitting on the trailer on the side of the interstate when the green flag drops! Things to consider for your hauler package include how far the racetrack is. The closer it is, the less of a rig you will need. What kind of races are you entering? For example, if you are racing a local Saturday night short track event, you don't need much. An open trailer and a halfway decent pickup will do the trick. If the distance of the event is significant, you are going to need a good tow vehicle, a 2500 series or better for most cars. Don't forget the amount of stuff you are going to load in the bed of the truck. It adds up! Four-wheel drive is not a necessity. You need a highway hauler, not a mud bog truck! You will also save money not opting for the 4x4 package.

Step Four—Trailer!

Now all you really need is an open car trailer, but again, depending on where and what you are racing, you may want to up the game. I have been to many single-day events that have left me baking in the sun or freezing my ball bearings off due to lack of shelter. For a little bit more money, you can find some decent enclosed trailers that will improve your quality of life and comfort during those long Mother Nature-challenged days. RV-type air-conditioning units will make life livable on those sweltering days. The enclosed trailer also makes life better when Jack Frost is beating you down or the rain begins to pour. Hopping into your race car after a rainstorm to find inches of water puddled in your seat makes for a long day! Put the car inside until the weather breaks!

Regardless of the type of trailer you choose, the most important part of trailering is safety. Load the trailer correct so the weight is balanced. There are many fine products made to stabilize a trailer's towing characteristics. Driving the rig home should not be a hair-raising experience but often is!

Yes, you need brakes! Don't skimp! Get a good electric brake controller. They can be a bit tricky to wire, so do what I do. Take your truck and trailer to an authorized installation center and tell them to make it stop. You will thank me later when you, your truck, trailer, race car, and whoever else was unfortunate enough to be riding with you. Don't end up in a ditch.

Special note: Please take care of your hauler and make sure it is in proper working order. Local police tend to prey on these vehicles and for good reason. I see too many rigs limp into the track that implicate that God does in fact perform miracles on a regular basis!

LESSON 3

Your First Race Car

Now that we have all of the needed support items in place, it is time to get a race car. A friend of mine read this and said, "All this time you've been shopping for trucks and trailers, you could have had the car ready by now."

This is possibly true, but in most cases, including my own limited budget team, it takes several months, if not years, to put it all together. During this time, the local rules package may change, and before you ever hit the track, your car is obsolete. Granted, if your budget is better than mine is, it is just a matter of driving to the local dealership to pick up a new dually, cruise on down to the local trailer dealer, and pick one out. Then roll out to the place you intend to race with a big wad of money in your pocket, walk up to the winner, and tell him to take his helmet and gloves. And you get the rest for that big wad of cash! Don't laugh! This is the best way to do it!

I do not suggest having a brand-new car built. Having a brand-new car does have the advantage of being state-of-the-art, brandy spanking-new, but that comes with a very high price tag. A car that cost $50,000 to build can be bought the following season for $15,000. The only market this doesn't seem to apply to is drag racing. Drag cars seem to hold value.

The most important fact of this is: do not build your own first car! Buy a used one and have a professional look it over. I have seen many proud owners of death traps that never should have been allowed to race.

For example, while racing a dirt track in North Carolina, I passed a fuel cell complete with fuel line laying on the front straight. No crash was around. It was just a fuel cell that fell out of somebody's car! Considering the craftsmanship involved with mounting the fuel cell, it makes me wonder how the seat and roll cage are mounted as well. Don't expect the track safety officials to look this stuff over. It's your life. Make sure you have it looked over.

Shop around and find a car that is turnkey for a good price. You can usually find a "roller" for next to nothing, but do not underestimate just how much outfitting that car can be. Pumps, pulleys, nuts, and bolts add up very quickly and usually to a very high amount. By purchasing a running race car, you get all of the parts and pieces required. You may—or more accurately, should—have everything rebuilt before you race it unless you are certain that everything is fresh. In the race car world, you will hear terms like, "only raced twice," "four hundred laps since rebuild," or "never bent." These comments are similar to "a little old lady drove it to church on Sunday." Let the buyer beware!

When you do purchase a race car, you don't want to let it out of your sight for long. What I am trying to say here is: don't strike a deal on Saturday, and go pick the car up several days later. That is how you wind up with a different chassis setup or engine than the car had when you agreed to purchase it.

Some Things to Look For When Buying a Race Car

Quality of welds is an indication of the fabrication quality. Once you start looking at welds, you will begin to notice a pattern that distinguishes the fabricator like a fingerprint. Working in shops with several people for a time, you can look at the work and tell who built what and who shouldn't be allowed to play with the welder!

Roll cage construction is critical, but more importantly, how it is attached to the car is the place overlooked. Many people will remove a professionally built roll cage from an existing car and put it into a different vehicle. If done properly, this is fine. However, I have seen some of the scariest footings on roll cages because this was not done properly. A roll cage should mount to the frame and not the floorboard in at least six locations. Certain production cars lack a distinctive frame. This type of chassis will require a large plate of steel under each leg of the main cage. One-eighth-inch-thick steel plates should be placed under the main uprights of the cage to secure the footings. This type of mounting is not acceptable in older street stock-type cars due to the age and condition of the floors.

The seat and belts will keep you alive and reduce injury in a crash. As long as your seat is mounted to the roll cage, wherever the cage goes, you follow. You should never have your seat mounted to the floor of the car. And what is just as bad is having the seat mounted to the cage and the belts not mounted to the cage. It all has to be one self-contained package. You, the seat, the belts, and the cage must be designed in such a way that you all move in unison.

The seat itself is a critical component. Positioning and containment is what you are after. Some very good economy seats are on the market that will contain you well. Obviously not as good as an SFI-rated seat, but for low-speed applications, it will work well. Don't get me wrong. This is not a place to cut corners; however, depending on the racing you are doing, an economy seat might be fine. Remember, it's your body and your life. You only get one. A cheap seat or one that does not fit properly can make a minor accident a major injury. Leg extensions, shoulder, and head supports are a must. A driver should be seated in the car with elbows and knees bent to prevent injuries during impact. (I call this the tuck-and-roll position.) Arms and legs straight out will flail about in a wreck and cause serious injuries by contact with the interior of the car. Pad everything!

The probability of fire is always underestimated. At a minimum, you need a three-layer, SFI-rated (or FIA-rated) suit. You should wear fire retardant underwear, and yes, I do understand that it is incredibly hot wearing four layers of protection. But again, depending on what you are racing, you may be able to use a two-layer suit. We must be concerned with the overall body temperature of the driver because heat injuries are no joke and can happen to anyone. Richard and Kyle Petty both struggled with heat injuries throughout their careers. If you have less than a three-layer suit, you must wear fireproof undergarments.

Make sure your floorboards are not full of holes where production components used to go through. Purpose-built race cars tend to not suffer from this problem as much as converted production cars, but more often than not, do not leave the seams unsealed, leaving space for fire to travel. Oval track, street stock cars, and production-based sports cars are likely to have many places that fire can get through to the interior of the car. Make sure you seal them up.

You need to be aware that fire in a race car is initially fueled by a superheated liquid that has been exposed to the atmosphere, typically after an impact causes a breach of integrity to the containment vessel. In layperson's terms, when you slam into something and bust open the fuel system or oiling system, all of that superheated liquid comes flying out under pressure and igniting on the way. If it lands on you, you are going to be on fire. With the exception of your oil pressure line, there should not be any liquid-filled lines in the driver compartment.

I understand this is nearly impossible with mid-tank cars, and in the case of such, I recommend a removable cover to contain the top of the tank. Never run a fuel pressure gauge inside the car unless it is a remote style. No fuel line should enter the driver's compartment. Do not use an inline fuel filter made of clear plastic or glass. These devices can crack from vibration and spray fuel into the engine compartment. Fram makes a very nice chassis-mounted fuel filter with replaceable element. All of the lines in your car should be Aeroquip, steel braided, or similar. No stock-type rubber hoses and no hard lines.

Go over your new race car carefully and remember, "When in doubt, throw it out!" If anything on your car is questionable, replace it with a new one. Don't be the guy who drops out of four straight events because of a fuel or ignition problem. Replace all questionable parts, and figure out what the problematic component was later.

Fire is pretty consistent regardless of the session. What I am saying here is: fire in practice is roughly the same temperature as it is in qualifying or the race. Wear all of your safety gear every time you drive. I know at least one of my readers is going to call me out for some high performance driving events (HPDE) where I wore a helmet, gloves, and a long-sleeved shirt. You know what? Stupid! That was a really dumb thing to do. And why did I do it? All the other guys were dressed that way, and I was stupid.

LESSON 4

Safety

There are three ways to be injured in a race car. Impact, intrusion, and fire.

Helmet

I am going to type this part in LARGE PRINT because this is the most important part of the book! YOUR HELMET MUST BE SNELL OR FIA-RATED! NO DOT HELMETS!

Your helmet must have this decal inside!

Do not allow your helmet to get banged up! Keep your helmet clean and in perfect condition. After a serious crash, the medical professionals will examine your helmet to help determine the nature of your injury. If your helmet is beat to crap because you mistreat it, it may have consequences. Even if the outer shell of your helmet is intact after a hard impact, you should replace it. The inner foam in the helmet will compress and not provide the same amount of energy absorption on your next impact. The helmet must have fireproof lining. The lining of a nonflame-resistant helmet will melt. Use your imagination what that will feel like.

Helmet Skirt

I prefer this option to a balaclava, but you must have one or the other to protect your neck from fire and, more importantly, to keep you from inhaling superheated air and flame.

Suit

Get a SFI 3-A5 or FIA equivalent. Wash it! An oil-soaked suit is no longer fire retardant. It is a fire accelerant! It must be in good condition. Holes in your suit make it useless. Get a new one every five years, if not sooner.

Undergarments

You should be wearing full-length, SFI-rated underwear. I understand that it is very hot and many of you will choose to not wear the underwear. If that is the case, understand the mechanics of your safety gear versus fire. Sweat steam creates a large amount of driver burns. Your sweat-soaked gear, when exposed to direct flame, will steam you like fresh vegetables. You must have layers between your skin and the suit. It's an outer layer, a first defense.

This label or FIA equivalent needs to be on all of your safety gear.

Gloves

You need them! Get them SFI or FIA–rated. If you are on fire, you are going to need your hands to get out. If you don't think you need gloves, try removing a pan from a hot oven without a pot holder. Fire is approximately 2,000 degrees Fahrenheit. If you don't understand this, you shouldn't be racing.

Shoes

Make sure they are SFI-rated.

Head and Neck Restraint

Make sure they are HANS or equivalent. Yes, you need one!

Hearing Protection

You must protect your hearing at all costs. In the car, I strongly suggest you have a racing communications company make your custom ear molds. The company can make the molds, or if more convenient, a local hearing aid/audiologist can make them and send them to the communications company. Repeat this process every five years because your ears never stop growing and it is important to have a perfect fit.

Belts

Make sure they are SFI-rated and new every two to three years. Make sure the belts are, at a minimum, five-point. Be sure to have these professionally installed. After a really bad crash, they should be replaced as well or sent to the manufacturer for recheck at the end of the season.

Window Net

It's the same as your belts. Make sure they are SFI-rated and new every two to three years.

Arm Restraints

If you can reach outside the roll cage of your car, you had better be wearing them.

Fire Suppression

You really need to have one of these. In all my years of racing, I have yet to see a driver use the mandatory fire extinguisher most places mandate. That doesn't mean it will never be needed. Anything can happen at any time. Spend the money on a good fire suppression system.

Fuel Cell

You must have a fuel cell with foam inserts and rollover devices such as a flap in the filler neck and a check valve in the vent line. Sports car guys are particularly guilty of using the factory fuel tank.

Seat

I talked a lot about the seat earlier in the book, but let's review. This must not be mounted to the floor. The seat needs to be mounted to the cage. No fiberglass or plastic. Aluminum or carbon fiber only. Head, shoulder, and side leg supports are needed. Make sure the seat is for you and not from someone who is a hundred pounds heavier than you are. You should be one with the seat.

Shop Safety

This area of racing is almost completely ignored. Ear and eye protection are mandatory. Dust mask or respirator should be in the shop and well maintained. No open-toe shoes! Fire extinguishers and first-aid kits should be readily available.

Interior Padding

Use SFI-rated padding inside the driver's compartment. Inferior padding will melt, burn, and drip. Wondering about yours? I am not telling you to set fire to anything, but I cut a small piece of padding off my car and put it in my fire pit out behind the house. Soon after, I changed the roll bar padding around my driver.

LESSON 5

Driving

Being a race car driver is much more than getting behind the wheel and driving fast. If you are going to be serious about performance, you must be a race car driver twenty-four hours per day and seven days per week. A healthy diet and strict physical training must be in place in order to achieve optimum performance. If you are out of shape, the physical demands of extreme heat, g-forces, and intense concentration will be nearly impossible to withstand in a long event. I have seen many drivers exit their race car after a twenty-lap oval race (about thirty minutes with cautions) looking physically exhausted. If you are wiped out after thirty minutes, you can't really expect to run the 500.

At this point, you have been to a school or two and spent several seasons at the racetrack watching what to do and what not to do. Now you can apply all of these great lessons. Stop here if you haven't been to a driving school or been raised by a racer who knows what he or she is talking about and has the résumé to back it up. It is important to understand that not every great driver can teach. Just because you can do it doesn't mean you can translate a talent into a lesson plan.

A difficult place for someone who has been raised by a racer is that you may have been taught wrong. This is a bad situation to be in because you may have some ingrained bad habits or, worse, misconceptions about racing. I see too many entry-level drivers who perform kill shots or take-out maneuvers on other competitors.

Let me say this. I have driven some of the fastest divisions on the tightest of tracks, all contact-free. There is no excuse for ramming another vehicle or deliberately wrecking someone else. Knocking another car out of the way is no different than a marathon runner tripping the competition. Actions of this nature degrade you, lessen the sport, and eventually come back and bite you. What comes around goes around. Race clean, and race hard. If you do make contact, it is what we call "rubbing," and in most forms of racing, a little rubbing is accepted. Slamming the car next to you is poor sportsmanship and hints at you overcoming a lack of talent or equipment quality. Pointing a fellow competitor toward the retaining wall at high speed is dangerous. Don't do it. If you think intentionally taking someone out is the way to compete, then please stop here and discard this book. I don't want anyone to think your mentality came from my tutorial.

Terminology and "Slang" Synonyms

- **Lock it down:** This is the first thing I teach any student. This is what you need to do once you have lost control of your car. Standing on the throttle of a car that has overrotated (spun out) to slow the car creates a more hazardous situation. You are only using two tires to stop the car and more than likely creating a cloud of tire smoke for everyone else to navigate through. Lock the brakes, and don't release them until you have stopped and all the other cars have passed by. If you can get the clutch depressed, great. Left foot brake drivers may find this difficult to do, but the most important part is the brake. Stalling the engine is nowhere near as bad as rolling into the path of an oncoming car.

- **Understeer (Slang: push, shove, tight):** The car is trying to go straight while you are trying to turn. "The car is pushing" means the car is understeering. This condition occurs when you are turning the wheel greater than the turning radius of the car. Understeer is when you hit the wall with the front of the car. When you are in an understeer condition, you have overloaded the front tires. Simply put, you are asking them to do too much in order to get the car to respond. Simply, you must demand less, and in return, the car will respond more. You need to turn less, slow down, release brake pressure, or do all of the above. You can experience understeer during acceleration if your car is not balanced properly. In this case, your only cure is to apply less throttle. If your car is not balanced properly, the only solution is to adjust the setup. Continuing to overdrive a car with an understeer condition can lead to brake and tire failure, potentially causing a dangerous situation. Do not continue to overdrive an ill-handling car. Fix it!
- **Oversteer: (Slang: loose, fishtailing, free):** Oversteer is when you put a minimal input into the wheel and get more rotation from the back of the car than the front. This may look cool and feel fast, but I assure you, regardless of what division you are racing in, the driver with the perfect amount of yaw to match the tire's slip angle is the fastest guy on the track. An exaggeration is the sport of drifting. When a car has excessive oversteer (when you hit the wall with the

back of the car), you really need to adjust the car to correct the balance. The driver's application of the throttle can correct some of that balance. When a car is oversteering, the back tires are not turning at the speed the car is traveling. In order to help reduce oversteer, you must apply enough throttle to match wheel rotation to distance traveled. With too little throttle, the car will overrotate (spin out) too much, and the same is likely. What is most important in an oversteer situation is to not overcorrect. An overcorrection on the wheel (turning the wheel too far) and reducing speed will send the car uncontrollably in the opposite direction. A good rule of thumb is to never go hand over hand when countersteering to compensate.

- **Pitch:** This is the angle or attitude the car has front to back under braking and acceleration. A lot can be learned about your race car by studying photos of your car entering, transitioning, and exiting turns. Compare these photos to other cars (specifically good running cars) in your division.
- **Roll:** This is the attitude of your car side to side or rather how much the car leans when going through a turn at speeds.
- **Yaw (Slang: four-wheel drift):** Yaw is the lateral direction the car is traveling. Think of an airplane that's flying a little sideways. The perfect yaw will equal the perfect slip angle of the tire.
- **Acceleration (Slang: bite, forward bite, drive):** This is the car's ability to accelerate in a straight line without spinning the tires.
- **Slip angle:** This is the direction the tire is moving in relation to the contact patch. A slip angle is a tire rolling forward with no lateral direction. The more

lateral direction you put on a tire, the greater the heat and wear will become. The type of tires and racing surface will determine the proper slip angle. A radial on pavement will maximize performance at eight to ten degrees of slip angle. A bias ply tire on a dirt surface will maximize performance considerably higher in the fifteen to twenty-degree angle. This is not a constant number due to varying conditions but very important to understand what slip does to a tire and how long it will last. In a long race, you want to drive well under the optimum slip angle to preserve the tires. In a short race, you may drive over the optimum slip angle because you don't have to worry about duration. Either way, too little or too much slip, you will not go as fast as you could be.

- **Zones:** There are several terms used to determine specific areas of the course you are competing on.
- **Approach**: This is the area typically at the end of a straight section of track. This can get complicated in linked turns where track out and approach get blurred together.
- **Brake zone:** This is the area of the course when you will be doing your hardest braking. You are off the throttle, downshifting, focused on hitting your mark, and heavy on the brakes. You may begin to turn in this section depending on the radius of the upcoming turn. Typically speaking, the tighter the turn, the less turning you will be doing in the area of the course and the heavier the braking. The brake zone is the area where brake rotors will begin to glow bright orange from the excessive heat. On a very wide turn or with lots of banking, you may brake all the way to the apex or possibly not at all. Simply letting off the accelerator

may be the amount of braking required to apex the turn.

- **Entry (Slang: turn in):** This is where you set the car into the turn. You should be releasing the brakes as you turn the wheel. You may be completely off the brake pedal, depending on how tight the turn is.
- **Apex:** This is the transitional part of the corner where you have completed slowing your car in order to make the turn, and then you begin accelerating. Your car should no longer be pitched forward from braking. It should be at its maximum roll. If possible, you should be accelerating through this part of the course, or rather just before the apex, you should lightly begin to apply the throttle. In most cases, you are stopping the braking effect of the engine. Many people feel, if you aren't braking, you should be accelerating, and they think this means using the pedals. Never forget when you lift your foot from the accelerator that this is in fact braking! The braking force generated will vary depending on the engine and its components. High RPM, high compression, and light rotating mass will break harder than heavy low RPM and low compression engines. Keep in mind that it is all rear brake and likely to cause a car to oversteer. You may need to adjust the brake bias to keep the car balanced. If this is the case, you will experience an oversteer condition at the end of the approach zone through the brake zone, and it will intensify at both the entry and the apex.
- **Track out (Slang: exit):** This is the area beyond the apex that you will be applying throttle as quickly as possible without causing an imbalance in the car's behavior. This is arguably the most important part of a turn. The one who gets to full throttle first typically

wins the race. Use the entire racetrack in this area to maximize your speed. One additional mile per hour gained in the track out area will exponentially multiply at the other end of the straight. That being said, losing one mile per hour will cause you to lose several at the other end of the straight. The age-old question of "What wins races, handling or horsepower?" is applied. The answer is straight-line speed. A good handling car will allow you to accelerate sooner, resulting in more straight-line speed. If you can figure out how to overcome handling issues with horsepower, you may have a shot! At one time I was driving for a team that had an ill-handling car with an enormous amount of horsepower. I focused the setup to track out and won many races with that car. In the braking zone, that car was evil. At the entry, it was possessed. But from the apex and through the track out area, it was capable of picking the inside front tire off the ground! Sometimes you have to sacrifice one area of the turn to focus on the strength of another area.

- **Radius:** This is a mathematical term for measuring an arc or circle. A tight radius is a tight turn; a wide radius is a big turn.
- **Decreasing radius:** This is a turn that gets tighter as you go. A decreasing radius will typically have a very late apex.
- **Increasing radius:** This is a turn that loosens up as you go. Increasing radius turns typically have a very early apex and make for hair-raising speeds once you accelerate out of the turn.
- **Banking:** This is the angle of the pavement relative to level. Daytona has a great amount of banking; Martinsville does not.

- **Cresting:** Some circuits have elevation changes that cause a crest or high point in the surface. Road courses are notorious for putting the fastest, most difficult apex on a crest, and to kick it up a notch, they commonly bank the pavement the opposite direction, also known as "off camber." If you look up the definition of "pucker factor," it will say "high speed off camber cresting apex." Check out turn ten at Virginia International Raceway.
- **Crowning:** This is your typical country lane where the center of the road is the highest point. If you apex very low in the turn, you have a small amount of banking. If you apex the turn wide, it will be off camber.
- **Flags:** Know your flags! Every series has a flagging system, but they are not all the same. You may even come across a flag you've never seen before. Check with your series for correct terminology. For example, a white flag from a road course corner worker does not mean "stand on it, one lap to go. It may mean there is a slow vehicle ahead, possibly a rescue vehicle or disabled race car."
- **Kinesthetic (Slang: your feel of the car):** This is an awareness of the position and movements of the car in relation to you by means of sensory organs in the muscles and joints. If you are in the back seat of a vehicle and cannot see out, you still comprehend when it begins to move, accelerate, turn, and brake.
- **Visual acuity:** Simply put, this is your vision and how much information your brain processes. Your peripheral vision is capable of processing a much larger amount opposed to your fixed vision.
- **Auditory awareness:** The sense of hearing is of great importance when driving a race car. Many times your rhythm or consistency driving a race car is greatly due

to what you hear. Knowing the exact exhaust note to alert you as to when to begin accelerating or braking, listening to tire noise as it changes from a low growl to a tortured squeal, or sensing the presence of another car's exhaust alert you to something you may not be able to see in the mirror or your peripheral vision.

Now that we have some basic terminology down, it is time to talk about driving! I shouldn't have to talk to you about car control because you have been to or are going to a school or two where professional instructors have taught or will teach you the do's and don'ts about car control. What I can tell you is the most important lesson I have ever learned is: if you are looking at it, you are going to hit it!

Look Ahead as Far Ahead as Possible at All Times!

Read that line again! Learn it! Live it! Love it! As long as you are looking ahead, your peripheral vision will take in all the needed information regarding space and distance to other cars and objects.

Hand position is very important, and I am assuming you have been taught or will be taught properly at driving school. Place two hands on the wheel! Do not ride around with your hand on the shifter unless you are drag racing. Even then, if time permits between gear shifts, you should always move your hand back to the correct position on the wheel.

Yes, I have seen some successful one-handed drivers, but I have also seen a man jump from an airplane without a parachute and land safely. I don't recommend either! You've heard "ten and two" or "nine and three." There are many different theories on this, but my suggestion is for your hands to be placed on the wheel just below shoulder height with your elbows bent at a forty-five-degree angle. By placing your hands at equal heights on the wheel, you will have an equal range of motion in both directions. Once you plant your hands on the wheel, they should never come off that position, especially in an oversteer correction situation. There are very few circumstances to override this statement. The only time a hand-over-hand correction should be attempted is at a very low speed because, at high speeds, it will cause an overcorrection situation, which will indeed end very badly both for you and anyone near you. If you find yourself having to go hand over hand, you are either overdriving your car or you have the wrong ratio steering. At which point, you will be standing on the brakes to reduce speed before impact.

LESSON 6

Marketing and Sponsorship

"How do I get sponsors?" If I had a nickel for every time I have heard that question, I would have enough money to run LeMans next year! Let's begin with what not to do.

What Not to Do

Don't beg for money on social media with statements like "sponsor needed or we can't finish the season." If this is your marketing plan, no one is going to take you seriously. Everyone will instead be thinking, "Oh, here is a company I would like to sink some money into. They're almost broke!"

"Sponsors wanted" is like a part-time job sign in front of a fast-food restaurant. It's just not the way to go. Or "I'll put your name on my car if you give me some money." Gee thanks! Can you write my name in the snow too? It's a partnership between you and—wait for it—your marketing partner. Please don't make your marketing pitch sound like you are panhandling. Let's move onto the do list.

What to Do

The appearance of your race car, hauler, shop, crew, and you all make a difference. If your car is beat up, your hauler is run-down, your shop is a crime scene, and your driver is scruffy and wearing rags for safety gear, this is not an attractive business anyone would want to invest in.

If your speaking voice sounds like you just crawled out from under an Appalachian rock, you are not going to keep the attention of anyone other than local folks who speak in kind. I understand we all come from different places and those places have diverse accents. In some ways, an accent is beneficial so don't be afraid to speak when you are outside your territory, but it is essential for you to speak well.

Product sponsorship is much easier to attain than monetary sponsorship. When you begin your marketing program, try to target businesses that may have services or products to barter. For example, I have an auto parts store as a partner who gives me discounted prices on parts. An auto body shop may straighten bent frame rails for free. I also have a machine shop and fabricator, both of which give me a significant discount when it comes to getting work done.

Don't be afraid to contact bigger organizations about products. I once had an agreement with a shoe company that supplied nothing but shoes, T-shirts, and a decal package for the car. It made my organization look so professional that sponsors came after me! Pizza shops, trucking companies, limousine companies, construction companies, auto parts distributors, and auto dealers all began approaching me with monetary offers because my team looked professional. I even had a hair salon offer to cut my hair, all for marketing space on the car.

Another big way to leverage marketing partners is alternative business, and I do see this often. It is referred to as "the rebate." Let's say, for example, I have an ice cream manufacturing business. Obviously milk is a key ingredient, and if I am going to make lots of ice cream, I am going to need lots of milk. I might express my dual interest for marketing partners for my race team while discussing how many thousands of gallons of milk I am going to buy from you for my ice cream business. Likely the term "rebate" will come up, meaning the supplying company will give your race team a rebate check at the end of the year for a percentage of your total purchasing.

One thing to be very careful about is what I call "the snake oil salesman." Several times during my career someone contacted me with lots of promises by dropping tons of big names and big plans. In the end, they will hit you up for a fee to get the ball rolling toward your dream sponsor, as the old saying goes, "If it sounds too good to be true, it probably is."

Don't get me wrong. There are some marketing people out there who will put together a nice PowerPoint presentation and do some social media exposure. In reality, it is not anything most of us aren't capable of doing on our own.

Marketing Recap

- Look the part! Be clean-cut and professional.
- Act the part! Arguing, fighting, cheating, or any other less than honorable actions on and off the track will tarnish your reputation.
- Write a résumé. Not everyone knows who you are or what you've done. A résumé is a quick and easy way to relay that information.
- Be prepared! Autograph cards, business cards, PowerPoint presentations, websites, and social media accounts are all very important. The first thing I always do when hiring or partnering is research via the Internet. If you tell me you are a professional race

car driver, then these are the things you should have, and I am going to look for them.

- Have a web domain. Buy your own name before someone else does. On that note, have you Googled yourself? You should because there could be someone with your same name and possibly doing things you don't want to be associated with. If you find someone with your same name, alter yours. Altering your name could be as simple as changing your competition name from "Joe" to "Joey." I started getting political messages through social media a few years back and realized there was a politician turned television host with the same name. I didn't change my name because I thought it was kind of cool. I wound up meeting a bunch of political activists accidentally. More fans for me!

EPILOGUE

If you have already begun racing or you are about to, you are entering the 1 percent of the population that has had the opportunity, dedication, and courage to climb into the cockpit of a race car. You will experience an avalanche of sensations and emotions, nervousness, nausea, heat fatigue, claustrophobia, muscle fatigue, pressure to perform, and moments of fear. If you are fortunate enough to experience the exhilaration of victory, you have entered the 1 percent of the 1 percent. Either way, welcome to a very exclusive club of modern-day chariot racing gladiators known as race car drivers.

I advise every student before competing for the first time to "look ahead and use your head. And wherever you finish today is the best finish you have ever had! Have fun!"

I hope you have enjoyed this book and come away with some good information. I cherish feedback, good or bad, so please feel free to contact me @http://www.joescarbrough.com !

Now go burn some rubber!

Printed in the United States
By Bookmasters